AF599457

by Nathan Sommer

Minneapolis, Minnesota

Credits

Cover, © Serhii Bobyk/Alamy Stock Photo, © Maryana Lyubenko/Alamy Stock Photo, © PA Images/Alamy Stock Photo, and © serhii/Adobe Stock; 4, © sturti/Getty Images; 4–5, © Anastasia Pelikh/Alamy Stock Photo; 6, © PatrikSlezak/iStock; 7, © sanjeri/iStock; 8, © shaunl/iStock; 9, © lev radin/Shutterstock; 10, © @diana_jarvis /Alamy Stock Photo; 11, © Tom Stack/Alamy Stock Photo; 12, © nimito/Adobe Stock; 12–13, © Paul Quezada-Neiman/Alamy Stock Photo; 14, © Arthur Cauty/Shutterstock; 15, © WWE / Contributor/Getty Images; 16, © Gregory__DUBUS/iStock; 17, © JJM Stock Photography/Travel/Alamy Stock Photo; 18, © Jennifer Graylock/Alamy Stock Photo; 19, © Photo 12/Alamy Stock Photo; 20, © Agencja Fotograficzna Caro/Alamy Stock Photo; 21, © Buff Henry Photography/Alamy Stock Photo; 22, © PA Images/Alamy Stock Photo; 22–23, © David Kleyn/Alamy Stock Photo; 24, © mrjo2405/iStock; 24–25, © Dragos Condrea/iStock; 26, © FilippoBacci/iStock; 27, © andresr/Getty Images; 28TL, © Antonio__Diaz/Getty Images; 28TR, © Mercedes Rancaño Otero/iStock; 28BL, © Paul Quezada-Neiman/Alamy Stock Photo; 28BR, © apilarinos/iStock; 29, © ZUMA Press Inc/Alamy Stock Photo; 31, © Sony Herdiana/iStock.

Bearport Publishing Company Product Development Team

Publisher: Jen Jenson; Director of Product Development: Spencer Brinker; Managing Editor: Allison Juda; Editor: Cole Nelson; Associate Editor: Naomi Reich; Associate Editor: Tiana Tran; Art Director: Colin O'Dea; Designer: Kim Jones; Designer: Kayla Eggert; Product Development Specialist: Owen Hamlin

Statement on Usage of Generative Artificial Intelligence

Bearport Publishing remains committed to publishing high-quality nonfiction books. Therefore, we restrict the use of generative AI to ensure accuracy of all text and visual components pertaining to a book's subject. See BearportPublishing.com for details.

Library of Congress Cataloging-in-Publication Data is available at www.loc.gov or upon request from the publisher.

ISBN: 979-8-89232-647-6 (hardcover)
ISBN: 979-8-89232-680-3 (ebook)

For more information, write to Bearport Publishing, 5357 Penn Avenue South, Minneapolis, MN 55419.

CONTENTS

An Entertaining Career 4

Leader of Rhythm: Choreographer 6

The Wackiest Crew: Circus Performer 8

Bringing the Past to Life: Historical Reenactor 10

Beastly Beautician: Special Effects Makeup Artist 12

Organized Chaos: Professional Wrestler 14

Explosion Expert: Pyrotechnician 16

Making a Scene: Set Designer 18

Danger Artist: Stunt Performer 20

Wild Rides: Amusement Park Designer 22

Creating the Impossible: Visual Effects Artist 24

Invisible Performer: Voice Actor 26

Living to Entertain 28

Entertainment Career Spotlight: Dwayne Johnson 29

Glossary 30

Read More 31

Learn More Online 31

Index 32

About the Author 32

AN ENTERTAINING CAREER

Turning on a movie, watching a live performance, or riding a roller coaster are fun ways to spend free time. However, for many people, entertainment is just another day at work. Across the world, people have developed careers around creating exciting experiences for others. It often takes hundreds of workers and months of preparation to get the job done. Are you ready to explore the world of entertainment careers?

The entertainment industry can be very competitive. People who choose careers in this field need to have lots of self-confidence to promote their skills and ideas.

LEADER OF RHYTHM

Choreographer

Behind every show-stopping dance performance is a great choreographer. These artists create routines that tell stories through movement. They work tirelessly to coach dancers of different ages and skill levels to prepare them for performances in concerts, plays, and films. Some choreographers specialize in creating non-dance routines for action scenes in movies and plays. They coordinate the movements of actors in staged fights to bring battles to life.

What It Takes

- ☑ Dance **expertise**
- ☑ Knowledge of different dance styles
- ☑ An ear for music and rhythm
- ☑ Leadership skills
- ☑ An ability to work long hours

Fight choreographers must be familiar with different styles of fighting, such as hand-to-hand combat and fencing.

Choreographers may coach many dancers at once or work with just a few.

The record for most backup dancers in one choreographed concert performance is 993!

THE WACKIEST CREW

Circus Performer

Circus performers put on jaw-dropping acts of bravery that astound audiences of all ages. They work hard to show off some of the most extraordinary—and sometimes dangerous—talents on Earth. Some performers swallow swords or juggle objects on fire. Others walk the tightrope or fly high above the crowd in **trapeze** performances. With only a few moments to wow the crowd, circus performers create shows unlike anything else!

What It Takes

- ☑ Circus arts training
- ☑ A love of traveling
- ☑ High energy
- ☑ The ability to work with others
- ☑ A **flexible** body

Sword swallowing is a very risky act that takes years of practice.

Injuries are common for circus performers. Statistically, **acrobats** have the most dangerous jobs in the show.

Trapeze artists are acrobats who perform stunts while flying through the air.

BRINGING THE PAST TO LIFE

Historical Reenactor

Historical reenactors pretend to be people from the past to educate and entertain audiences of the present. They may act out historical scenes of everyday life or important events, such as famous military battles. These actors study hard to accurately portray people from a different time. They dress in **period** clothing and speak with historical **dialects**. They often interact with audience members, answering questions to give a richer view of the past.

What It Takes

- ✓ A love of history
- ✓ Acting skills
- ✓ The ability to stay in character for many hours
- ✓ The careful use of old tools and weapons

Some reenactors work as guides in historical villages or museums.

Battle performances can have hundreds or thousands of reenactors.

Many historical reenactors are **volunteers**. They aren't paid, but they do the job because they love history.

BEASTLY BEAUTICIAN

Special Effects Makeup Artist

Who helps when actors need to become superheroes, zombies, or unusual creatures? Special effects makeup artists are up for the job! These experts combine makeup with **prosthetics**, masks, and other materials to complete wild transformations. They can create the appearance of realistic-looking injuries or turn actors into creepy unearthly beings. Once special effects makeup is applied, these artists stay nearby to provide touch-ups and keep actors looking their best . . . or their creepiest!

What It Takes

- ☑ A cosmetology degree
- ☑ Steady hands
- ☑ Patience
- ☑ The ability to make things look realistic
- ☑ Prosthetics knowledge

These makeup artists apply many layers of glue and other materials to create realistic wounds.

Makeup artists use prosthetics to change the shape of an actor's face and body.

It can take as long as 20 hours to complete detailed special effects makeup.

ORGANIZED CHAOS

Professional Wrestler

Professional wrestlers combine acting and athleticism to put on over-the-top **scripted** fights. They play characters in the storyline of the fight and work together to act out choreographed stunts, such as body slams, dives, and backflips. Pro wrestlers spend hours practicing their moves for these planned performances. This allows them to stay in character and even **improvise** to create more drama for the crowd.

What It Takes

- ☑ A professional wrestling school certificate
- ☑ Physical fitness
- ☑ Improvisation skills
- ☑ A high pain tolerance
- ☑ The ability to handle boos from the crowd

In the storyline of a match, pro wrestlers play different roles. The villain character is called a heel, and the good guy is the face.

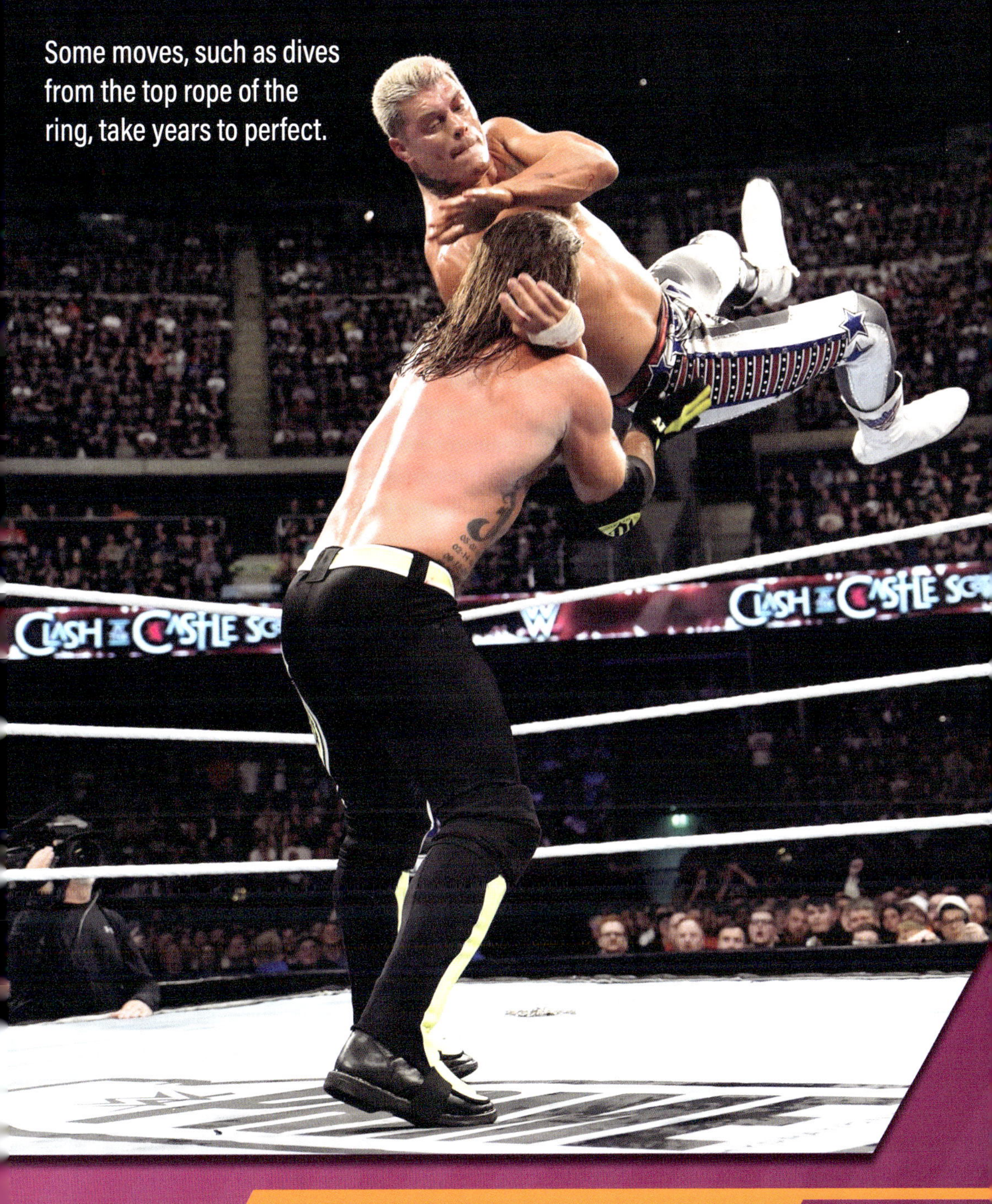

Some moves, such as dives from the top rope of the ring, take years to perfect.

Professional wrestlers need to be comfortable in front of crowds. Sometimes, more than 100,000 people attend these events!

EXPLOSION EXPERT

Pyrotechnician

How would you like to blow things up for a living? Pyrotechnicians design, build, and oversee the safe **detonation** of controlled explosions. They are responsible for the bombs, blasts, fires, and flying bullet effects in movies and TV shows. Some pyrotechnicians also create firework displays for oohing and aahing crowds. While pyrotechnicians aim to put on incredible displays, they must also make safety a priority. These experts create detailed plans for each explosion.

What It Takes

- ☑ A pyrotechnics license
- ☑ Safety training
- ☑ Expertise in chemical reactions
- ☑ Careful planning
- ☑ A willingness to work in all types of weather

Pyrotechnicians can create huge shows with more than 500,000 fireworks.

Pyrotechnicians must be tech-savvy. Most large displays are controlled by computers.

Pyrotechnicians create fireballs and other effects for explosions in movies.

MAKING A SCENE

Set Designer

Set designers create the ideas for the awe-inspiring worlds of movies, TV shows, and plays. They are tasked with sketching, drawing, and overseeing the construction of each set. They also work with directors and other members of the production team to make sure each set works for the whole story. Once the sets are built, these designers select and arrange props, furniture, and other elements to make the scenery come to life.

What It Takes

- ☑ Architecture or interior design experience
- ☑ An eye for detail
- ☑ An ability to think outside the box
- ☑ Good communication skills

Sometimes, set designers make small models of their designs to make sure everything looks good.

Set designers may transform places that already exist or sketch new sets that will be built from scratch.

Set designers carefully read scripts to gather details about the worlds they are creating.

DANGER ARTIST

Stunt Performer

Flipping, flying, falling, and taking a punch are all in a day's work for stunt performers. These highly trained professionals plan and safely perform stunts in films and plays. Sometimes, they work as **body doubles**. This means they complete dangerous stunts in place of actors. Carefully planned camera angles help hide the swap from audiences. These daring workers use harnesses, giant airbags, and other tools to avoid injuries during thrilling action scenes.

What It Takes

- ☑ Safety training
- ☑ Specialized skills, such as fighting, falling, or driving
- ☑ A calm head in dangerous situations
- ☑ An ability to work in all kinds of weather
- ☑ Energy and persistence

Special fireproof clothing helps keep performers protected during fire stunts.

Sometimes, a stunt performer's job is to jump and fall from great heights.

Many stunts last for only a few seconds. However, preparing for them can take days of practice!

Amusement Park Designer

Amusement park designers are paid to create fun! They plan and sketch the layout of amusement parks. These designers also come up with new ideas for extreme rides and attractions that are sure to wow any visitor. They must make sure their parks provide maximum thrills while remaining completely safe. It takes a lot of time and planning to create exciting moments of fun for others.

What It Takes

- ☑ An engineering or architecture degree
- ☑ Excellent illustration skills
- ☑ Knowledge of safety laws
- ☑ Good time management
- ☑ A love for amusement parks

Some designers have started combining roller coasters with **virtual reality** headsets.

Amusement park designers create coasters to be both exciting to ride and cool to look at.

After these park designers have done their work, it may still take years before the park is up and running.

CREATING THE IMPOSSIBLE

Visual Effects Artist

Visual effects artists work to make the impossible details in movies and videos appear real. These artists use computers to create creatures, **environments**, and much more. This computer-generated imagery, or CGI, is then added to various media for stunning, realistic results. To make a video as perfect as possible, visual effects artists also use CGI to remove unwanted details or adjust aspects of the film, such as color and lighting.

What It Takes

- ☑ A graphic design degree
- ☑ Expertise in visual effects software
- ☑ An eye for detail
- ☑ Creativity
- ☑ A passion for visual effects
- ☑ The ability to meet tight deadlines

Visual effects artists get lots of feedback before a piece of CGI is finalized.

It can take visual effects artists more than an hour to create a minute of screen effects.

Many visual effects artists use **artificial intelligence** to help them work faster.

INVISIBLE PERFORMER

Voice Actor

Many actors use their bodies to show emotion, but some do this with just their voices! Voice actors work behind microphones to **narrate** or play animated characters in films, TV shows, video games, and more. Sometimes, they may play a variety of roles, changing their voice and speaking with a different accent for each character. These unseen performers do more than just speak—they also shout, gasp, and grunt as their on-screen characters struggle or move.

What It Takes

- ☑ Acting experience
- ☑ Knowledge of microphone techniques
- ☑ The ability to speak clearly
- ☑ A wide vocal range

Sometimes, voice actors use audio equipment to record and edit their work.

Voice actors often record their lines many times in different ways.

Voice actors record the speech for toys, audiobooks, and **GPS** devices.

LIVING TO ENTERTAIN

People who choose exciting careers in entertainment are often very passionate about their work. Whether dancing, acting, designing, or flying through the air, these artists provide audiences with an escape from everyday life. A career in entertainment might not always be glamorous, but it is fun and rewarding work!

ENTERTAINMENT CAREER SPOTLIGHT

Dwayne Johnson

Dwayne Johnson got his start as a professional wrestler. Playing the character of The Rock, he won the World Wrestling Entertainment Championship eight times. Fans quickly fell in love with Johnson's **charisma**. Soon, he began a career acting in movies. He has also been a voice actor in films and video games, including *Moana*, *DC League of Super-Pets*, and *Fortnite*.

GLOSSARY

acrobats athletes who perform exciting gymnastic acts

artificial intelligence computer programs that can think, learn, and perform the tasks of people

body doubles performers who take the place of actors in certain scenes

charisma a special charm or appeal

detonation the act of causing a bomb to explode

dialects the ways languages are spoken from certain areas or times in history

environments the surroundings of specific places

expertise specialty knowledge or skills on a subject

flexible able to move and bend easily

GPS Global Positioning System; a navigation system that uses satellites to provide accurate location information

improvise to act or give a speech without preparation

narrate to tell a story or speak the words in a program

period relating to a particular time in history

prosthetics artificial body parts used to change the look of an actor's face and body

scripted planned action of performances

trapeze a type of acrobatics in which performers swing from a horizontal bar high above ground

virtual reality a fake world made by computers that looks and sounds real

volunteers people who do work without getting paid

READ MORE

Doeden, Matt. *Dwayne "The Rock" Johnson: From Wrestler to Hollywood Hero (Gateway Biographies).* Minneapolis: Lerner Publications, 2023.

Gobin, Shantel. *Careers in the Studio (Design Your Future).* Vero Beach, FL: Rourke, 2023.

Murray, Laura K. *Making Movies (Making Media).* Minneapolis: Abdo Publishing, 2024.

LEARN MORE ONLINE

1. Go to **FactSurfer.com** or scan the QR code below.

2. Enter "**Entertainment Careers**" into the search box.

3. Click on the cover of this book to see a list of websites.

INDEX

actors 6, 10, 12–13, 20, 26–27
artificial intelligence 25
battles 6, 10–11
characters 10, 14, 26, 29
computer 17, 24
concerts 6–7
creatures 12, 24
dance 6
explosions 16–17
fighting 6, 14 20
fireworks 16
history 10–11
injuries 9, 12, 20
Johnson, Dwayne 29
makeup 12–13
movies 6, 16–18, 24, 29
plays 6, 18, 20
prosthetics 12–13
roller coaster 4, 23
safety 16, 20, 22
set 18–19
special effects 12–13
stunts 9, 14, 20–21
TV 16, 18, 26
wrestling 14–15, 29

ABOUT THE AUTHOR

Nathan Sommer graduated from the University of Minnesota with degrees in journalism and political science. In his free time, he enjoys camping, hiking, and writing. Nathan lives in Minneapolis, Minnesota.